How America Died

A Letter to the Future

Tim Hall

First Printing – July 2009

This is copy 17 of 25

Undie Press

How America Died:

A Letter to the Future

ISBN: 978-0-9763460-6-7

Undie Press
PO Box 13
Wayne, IL 60184

For volume discounts of this title (5 or more copies) please email
TimHallBooks@gmail.com.

Printed in the USA

THIS IS A LIVING BOOK.

You can help write it. See info at the back.

Introduction

This is not a political book.

How America Died is my attempt to answer the question, "What is control?" By control I do not mean authority or laws, at least not necessarily, but rather the act of dominating or coercing, through threats or outright destruction, another human being. Where does this urge come from, and how does it spread?

In an attempt to isolate and identify the mechanism of control I've drawn from a number of medical, psychological, and sociological theories, and reconstructed them in what I hope is an original and entertaining way. I cannot vouch for the scientific validity of these theories, or even be sure of my own interpretation of them; all I can say for sure is that they have helped me a great deal in recent years, especially when trying to understand some of the unpleasant extremes of human behavior. I wrote this book under the assumption that perhaps other people out there might also be searching for similar answers. This is not meant to be an authoritative or comprehensive treatise on the subject of control, but as a starting point for your own explorations and research.

Although I have made every effort to credit my sources in the text, several writers deserve special thanks: William S. Burroughs, for his visionary ideas about control and the language virus; Richard Dawkins and Richard Brodie, for their groundbreaking work on memes and selfish genes; and Sam Vaknin, for his brave and insightful work on pathological narcissism.

This book would not have been possible without the work of these individuals, and the bulk of the credit for any helpful insights contained herein must first go to them. I must also stress that while this book was inspired by and synthesized from many sources, it does not in any way represent the conclusions, opinions, or views of any other individual or group.

In other words, any good parts in this book are probably thanks to someone else; the bad parts are entirely mine.

Tim Hall
June 2009

Table of Contents

Introduction

A Letter To The Future

Dear Children of the Future:

I am writing today to tell you how America died. I take no pleasure in these words, and wish I did not have to write them, but it occurs to me that somebody, somewhere, at some point in the future might want to know a little bit about what happened to us, since I assume that all you will have available to you is the official version, and as you are no doubt aware the official version has only ever served one purpose throughout history: not offending those in power.

I'm sorry we will not have a chance to meet, but I like to imagine that your world is not much different from mine. I find it comforting to dream that the world is better where you are, and yet somehow familiar to me. I see you in your classrooms of the future, and note that the entire educational enterprise is still basically a forlorn, exasperating experience for all involved. Schools still need more money. Children are still occasionally cruel to other children, no matter how extreme the threat of official violence that hangs over them. They are also, I'm sure, the same wonderful, wide-eyed, innocent creatures of today. Teachers are still the overworked, underpaid, slightly grubby angels faced with the unenviable task of trying to convince you that sitting in those stifling rooms and rude chairs, day after day, is actually better for you than running wild through the world, as I know most of you would prefer.

Of course, I can imagine that many things have not necessarily changed for the better. I can just as easily imagine that your lives are more difficult in many ways, festooned with an array of fiendishly clever new devices for regulating your every mood, thought, attitude and action.

It's not much a stretch, since by the end of America we had become experts in the legislative and technological bondage of our people. Very often the art of speculative writing is really little more than buying the present a bigger set of clothes.

I can see you living in a world where you are not allowed to venture into a body of water unless equipped with the proper flotation devices; I can see a world where it is against the law to question the official record. I can see laws requiring people to wear lighted clothing at night, and for cars to keep their headlights on even when parked. I can see politicians giving speeches about the evils of tobacco years after it has been outlawed, even as the sea levels continue to rise, ice caps melt and cancer rates skyrocket around the world. I can see a world where it will be a felony for children to refuse to buy certain products, or state-mandated medication.

I can see all of these things because many of them are already coming to pass.

At the time I am writing this America has not yet failed. Our mechanical society still functions more or less as it has for at least a century: people still have jobs, cars move along the highways, business is conducted in a generally civil manner by mostly decent people.

These outward signs are comforting, but also illusory. America has in fact reached one of those points in its history when a perfect storm of events has converged—political, economic, military and diplomatic—and, rather than meet these challenges responsibly, the country has once again responded by going insane. The question many people are asking now is: Is this the last time? Will we be lucky enough to pull ourselves out of this, at least without sparking a global war and wiping out millions of lives in the process?

America has had any number of tantrums and breakdowns throughout her short history, just like any beautiful, vain, and insecure child might. It is also a nation whose politicians and pundits believe, again like a child might, that to have experienced the dumb luck of being born in a specific geographical location shows empirically that one is superior to the rest of the world; and that the world ignored our tantrums at its peril. Despite our radically increased dependence on other parts of the world in recent decades—the Middle East for oil, China for cheap labor, for example—or perhaps because of it, many of my fellow countrymen and women live with the unshakable faith that we are not only objectively but *innately* superior to other human beings, simply by virtue of having been "American." No matter what the circumstances or conditions, no matter how depraved, cruel, or deceptive our behavior, we came to believe that if it was done by American power then it was, by definition, good.

Again, this was as old as America. From the manifest destiny of the pioneer and frontier days to the exceptionalism of present times, we came to believe that the experience of stepping off a boat as strangers in a strange land was somehow different, better, more *right* if done by certain people. We came to believe that this was okay, because God blessed us with an abundance that, once squandered, did nothing to cure us of our self-regard. Americans have always had their hands pressed together in prayer; the problem is that in recent decades our fingers have not been pointing towards God, but to our own faces. America might claim devotion to God, but she prays only to herself.

This seemingly bottomless capacity for self-regard is one thing in a child; it is something else altogether in a heavily armed, bankrupt, and energy-poor nation like America, capable of causing enormous destruction and even extinction on a planetary level. And I believe—and this is why I am writing this to you now—that the conditions leading to our collapse have been caused by one thing: an invisible killer that we refused to acknowledge, not because we were blind to it or in denial, but because we wanted it to succeed. In other words, we died because we wanted to. We just didn't realize it.

Before I explain what I mean, I'd like to give you children of the future a snapshot of what is happening in America right now, in March of 2009, as I sit down to write this.

Financial terrorists have taken control of our money system, destroying not only our own economy but also the economies of many other nations around the world. These terrorists have not only refused to accept responsibility for their actions, but have in fact threatened the people with bigger and greater destruction unless we continue to pay them exorbitant sums, and hold them blameless for these and any other acts of terrorism they choose to commit in the future.

Our democratically elected leaders have seized control of all communications within our borders without our consent: all mail, emails, text messages, and phone calls are now the legal property of the state, which has claimed the power to divert and examine them in secret, at will, for any reason. If that weren't enough the government has asserted it has the right to arbitrarily snatch, torture, and detain anybody, at any time, and hold them forever, without charges or trial.

These are not the policies of one party, administration, or rogue element within our government, but have been enthusiastically endorsed by both political parties as well as their many advisors, media outlets, and corporate interests.

As I write this, in the spring of 2009, there is literally not one area of our lives over which the government does not now claim absolute and total power. There is no longer any meaningful difference between our various police, enforcement, spying, and military groups. The two-party system has failed. For the last 60 years conservatives have been marching us in lockstep over the edge of a cliff; during that time liberals have been arguing that it would be better to march us into caves instead, and simply bring the mountain down on top of us.

Television programs form our ideas of justice: we are inundated with soap operas of punishment, from the cartoon judges and shame-based confessionals of morning television to the voyeuristic operettas of evening crime dramas and bloody surgical reenactments. We have national leaders who have repeatedly referred to a fictional television character, Jack Bauer, as the standard-bearer for American foreign and military policy.

Our lives are in the hands of the most powerful drug cartels in history, huge pharmaceutical companies whose mission is to prevent cures from ever coming to market and who enjoy immunity from prosecution for even their most toxic and deadly concoctions. Whatever naturally occurring vitamins, remedies, and drugs the cartels cannot patent have either already been, or else are in the process of being, criminalized.

Our food is in the hands of huge factory farms that are notorious for their filthy, diseased, and cruel conditions, and yet have recently created legislation that requires small, organic farms to implant livestock with expensive microchips, but which exempts themselves.[1]

Our faith is in the hands of religious fanatics who, instead of being humbled and awed by the amazing diversity of life on earth, have convinced themselves that God has chosen them to impose only two possible paths on the rest of us: their way, or death.

We are ruled on all sides by perverts, adulterers, rapists, pedophiles, embezzlers, tax cheats, draft dodgers, drug addicts and alcoholics, who nevertheless lecture us from podiums about our common moral good, our national character, the shining beacon of hope we offer the world. They preach the gospel of a great and glorious exceptionalism, the creed of American Supremacy that justifies our every act of greed, cowardice, and violence.

In order to feel anything in our spied-upon, increasingly unsafe, government-mediated and drug-dulled lives, we have resorted to hanging myriad technological gadgets on our bodies, un-

---

[1]http://libertarianrepublican.blogspot.com/2009/05/how-big-brother-agribusiness-will-get.html

der the bizarre belief that they are essential for our survival and somehow increase our freedom. I cannot help but notice that most of these gadgets, bought and subscribed to in the name of "staying in touch," actually allow us to be farther away from each other for longer periods.

In other words, everything is exactly as it has been for a long time.

History, at least of the classroom variety, is better at explaining what happened rather than how or why. The hows and whys tend to involve responsibility or even blame, and in our misguided decency we have virtually outlawed such discussions in the classroom, at least where our power centers are concerned. I mention this only because the conditions that brought about our end were therefore visible for some time, but we were trained to believe that these were irritating anomalies, that our lives would always return to prosperity and happiness on their own, that justice and truth were immutable laws of the universe rather than fragile, hated ideals that had to be zealously guarded and fought for.

We were nothing if not *optimistic*.

Oh, children of the future! If I could convince you to be on your guard against only two types of people, it would be those who are optimistic about the future, and those who are nostalgic for the past. Both yearn for things that do not, never have, or will ever exist; neither will admit, in his glorious conception of imaginary times, how he is helping to make the present so much worse by comparison.

How America Died

Now that I have told you a little bit about what America was like at the end, I can tell you how she died.

A virus.

I am not talking about a poetic or meta-phorical virus, per se; it is not a "virus of the mind" or psychopathology, at least not exactly. I believe it is a real, physical, *literal* virus, airborne and quantifiable. Most of us have been infected with it at some point in our lives, but as with childhood illnesses most of us developed antibod-ies to resist the virus. Weaker individuals, however, became permanently infected and lived among us, undiagnosed and untreated, until the virus was able to evolve and mutate into forms that could infect all of us.

The virus I am talking about is very common and very old; it has killed countless millions throughout history, as well as every great empire or civilization. The virus has started every war in human history, has committed every act of violence, mayhem, and destruction. It is such a threat that mankind developed many complex strategies for dealing with it over the years in order preserve society, to no avail.

America, like every other civilization that has fallen to the virus, thought it was different.

The virus is not an ideology, philosophy, religion or political affiliation. It is not based on class, race, gender or dietary preference. It grew steadily and silently through the years, aided and abetted, nurtured and spread by small clusters of infected individuals until it had infiltrated our economy, military, politicians and media—not even our artists and academic institutions could resist it.

The virus is not Evil, at least not in the way we think of the word, though people under the influence of the virus are responsible for most if not all of the evil we see in the world.

The virus is control.

It is my belief that control—specifically, the desire to dominate or destroy others—is a *biological* condition, one that has been spread by individuals, groups, or entire nations into other people or populations by the same methods throughout history, regardless of culture, religion, political or economic systems.

I am not talking about the systems of control that we all need to a certain degree: parental authority, business hierarchies, military discipline, or the self-control of athletes, for example. Control systems are necessary, whether to achieve personal greatness or to maintain a functioning and healthy social order.

Healthy control systems become infected when they cease using control in the service of self-discipline and instead focus on dominating and destroying others. When this happens then these systems are no longer operational in any standard sense of the word but instead are simulations, operated by the control virus.

The control virus comes in many forms, but almost always infects people in the same way:

physical contact, via the sensory organs, from exposure to trauma. The trauma can be visual, auditory, or subcutaneous. The most common infection point is childhood, the time of life when we are most susceptible to beatings, sexual assault, verbal and emotional abuse; however a child can become infected through any long-term exposure to excessive levels of control (needy/smothering/doting parents can do just as much harm as cold/neglectful/abusive ones, for example). Infection levels vary widely, depending on the amount and severity of contact. The control virus can sicken healthy adults, but most recover. I believe the only adults who become permanently infected are those who have had some kind of severe earlier exposure, which is triggered by a later experience with trauma.

Those who have suffered catastrophic control infections generally fall into two camps, which I will call carriers and shrinkers.

Carriers of the control virus are common enough in our society that we already have names for them. We call such carriers control freaks, control addicts, or even vampires. (Those of you who don't know the story behind *Dracula* might be interested to learn that it was written while Bram Stoker was working as a business manager for a theater in London; the character Dracula was based on the insufferably stiff, vain, controlling and abusive lead actor at the theater, to whom Stoker then presented the finished story as a role for him to play—making *Dracula* not only one of the first (and still finest) examples of the control virus in literature, but also one of the ballsiest acts of literary gamesmanship against a living vampire ever attempted.)

The second group, the shrinkers, are those individuals who have suffered severe exposure to the control virus but who fight back from full infection. I believe that the most well known of the shrinkers are those suffering from post-traumatic stress disorder, or PTSD.

New research has discovered possible genetic links to certain manifestations of the infection: some personality disorders have been found to have genetic markers[2], for example. Other research has shed light on the neuroanatomy of PTSD[3]. In a recent study, soldiers with PTSD

---

[2] British Journal of Psychiatry, 160: 12-23 (1992). "The genetics of personality disorders." Retrieved from:

http://bjp.rcpsych.org/cgi/content/abstract/160/1/12

[3] JAMA. "Association of FKBP5 polymorphisms and childhood abuse with risk of posttraumatic stress disorder symptoms in adults." 18 Mar 2008.

were found to have hippocampuses that were as much as 20% smaller on average when compared with their peers; the study also revealed that the chemicals released along the hypothalamus-pituitary-adrenal (HPA) axis were significantly different than non-sufferers.

Although more research must be done, these studies suggest that witnessing traumatic event may cause severe, even permanent, *physical* damage. I believe that it is only a matter of time before we discover that trauma not only triggers genetic mutations, but in fact causes them.

As a result of these studies, as well as my own detailed observations over the years, I have also come to believe that most of the personality disorders that are described by the DSM-IV as Type II—including borderline, narcissistic, histrionic and the like—are not really "personality" disorders at all, but can be better described as *control* disorders. Individuals with these disorders are primarily concerned with controlling the behavior of others, through constant threats, drama, self-victimization, and a steadfast refusal to accept responsibility their own actions. They are masters at manipulating those around them, and over time can become extremely adept at spreading the control virus, creating so much chaos and pain that after prolonged exposure to a control addict even formerly healthy individuals can become very sick and debilitated.

Control addicts are carriers of the control virus, but it is important to note that *they are not the virus itself.* People are not pathologies; however I believe they can be subsumed by pathologies far more than previously believed. The trauma that triggers such disorders erases boundaries, destroys the healthy ego—makes the abused, in effect, a hollowed-out shell for the virus to inhabit and animate. In fact, I believe that most of the primary symptoms of personality disorders (whether grandiosity, suicidal ideation, extreme sense of entitlement, sexual opportunism, etc.) are in fact *secondary* characteristics of the control virus, and that these severe control disorders are bound by a different common goal, which I will explain shortly.

Control addicts are often thought, in the larger sense, to be suffering from a dissociative disorder of some sort, but this is too generic, as we are all capable of dissociating in mild ways: "becoming numb" when confronted with a shocking or traumatic event, for example, or "losing" ourselves in a good book or movie.[4]

The popular, Freudian view of extreme dissociation is that it is a form of psychological defense, but French psychiatrist Pierre Janet disagreed. Janet argued that the act of dissociation was not a psychological defense, but a *constitutional weakness*.[5] If true, then this would also indicate that control is a *physical* problem more than a psychological one. As one of the great chroniclers of Type II personality disorders, Sam Vaknin, wrote:

> The three authors of the Dimensional Assessment of Personality Pathology (Livesley, Jackson, and Schroeder) joined forces with Jang in 1993 to study whether 18 of the personality dimensions were heritable. They found that 40 to 60% of the recurrence of certain personality traits across generations can be explained by heredity: anxiousness, callousness, cognitive distortion, compulsivity, identity problems,

---

[4]Source: http://www.sidran.org/
[5]Pierre Janet, *The Mental State of Hystericals* (1893)

oppositionality, rejection, restricted expression, social avoidance, stimulus seeking, and suspiciousness. Each and every one of these qualities is associated with a personality disorder. In a roundabout way, therefore, this study supports the hypothesis that personality disorders are hereditary.

This would go a long way towards explaining why in the same family, with the same set of parents and an identical emotional environment, some siblings grow to have personality disorders, while others are perfectly "normal". Surely, this indicates a genetic predisposition of some people to developing personality disorders.[6]

If susceptibility to the control virus is in fact genetic, and triggered by sensory trauma, then the selfish gene theory of Richard Dawkins[7] would suggest that infection turns individuals into nothing more than genetic survival machines for the virus—dedicating themselves,

---

[6] Vaknin, Sam. "Genetics And Personality Disorders." Chronicle Online, Oct. 15, 2006. Retrieved from:
http://www.americanchronicle.com/articles/view/14889
[7] *The Selfish Gene*, 1976.

indirectly and unknowingly, to the protection and advancement of the control virus.

If this is true, and if stress disorders, certain neuroses and even addictions are found to be crude attempts to self-medicate against genetic mutation and infection from the control virus, then it is entirely possible that there are many other control-related disorders, or that these mutations are themselves mutating into other illnesses that to date have no known cause. Therefore autism, diabetes or even obesity—especially in those individuals with no family history of these conditions—might one day be traced back to some ancestral legacy of abuse or trauma from generations past.

I realize this premise—that the need to dominate and destroy others is a communicable disease brought about by the genetic mutation caused by a virus—might seem not only absurd but reductive, minimizing or denying personal responsibility for our actions or health. Not at all. The discovery of the first virus a century ago didn't reduce the need for hygiene but greatly increased it. Identifying and isolating the agent of control will only lead to a more rigorous understanding of health and hygiene that will benefit us all. What the discovery of the first virus did, most importantly, was to dampen the influence of those scolds and finger-pointers who until then believed that disease and vice were the result of moral failings or Divine Providence.

Such a discovery would be a cause for rejoicing: it would mean that in the future there might very well be an antidote for evil.

Introducing The Vyron

In order to differentiate the control virus from the ones that cause the common cold or shingles I will refer to it as the Vyron. The Vyron is the unit of control, the contagious particle of domination, the irreducible element of destruction.

Since the Vyron creates the need to dominate, threaten, and destroy others in those it infects it naturally hates any person or idea that promotes harmony and peace. The Vyron therefore hates community, family, happiness, tolerance, security, and justice.

The Vyron is non-partisan and does not discriminate against who it infects. It has no intelligence or ideas of its own; like all viruses the Vyron is stupid, dull, barely alive. Instead the

Vyron uses an infected person's intelligence and passions for its own aims.

It has no power except through the process of animating the host. Power is potential. The desire to accumulate power is a natural human instinct, and can serve as good protection against the control virus (most personality/control disorders begin as defense mechanisms, in fact). Of course, the sad irony is that power itself attracts the virus, making the need for more power and wealth (for further protection) a somewhat self-fulfilling prophecy. The virus needs power in order to spread more effectively, as power allows it to inflict trauma, and therefore further infection, against others.

To put it another way: Power infects, and absolute power infects absolutely.

Memes & The Vyron

To help understand the Vyron I must first distinguish it from memes. Richard Dawkins, who I mentioned earlier, discovered and coined the meme. Simply put, the meme is to culture what the gene is to biology; it is the unit of cultural transmission. Anything that can replicate itself through society—songs, brand names, advertising and political slogans, even entire philosophies—can be described as memes. More complex memes are themselves comprised of memeplexes, or a lexicon of sub-memes devoted to that larger meme. Therefore, astrology is a meme but also describes a memeplex that itself includes the memes of "rising sign," "Aries," "horoscope," etc.

Richard Brodie, another prominent meme researcher, calls memes "viruses" (*Virus Of The Mind*), so I want to distinguish between memes and what I call the control virus.

Memes and the control virus can both be said to be contagious, but the concept of the meme refers more to a kind of a delivery device for cultural or linguistic evolution, whereas the control virus *actually changes the physiology* of those infected. I also think it is incorrect to think of control as a concept, idea, or goal; it is an *act*, and therefore falls outside memetics as I understand it. In other words, the word "Vyron" is a meme, but the epidemiology of the control virus is not. Many of the justifications for control are memes: wealth, power, fame, family values, Life, Death, victory—but not Control itself, which is the *act* of dominating or destroying others. Control is a physical, literal reality, which is perhaps why, in our increasingly abstracted, remote-controlled society of meme proxies, the word "Control" is almost never uttered by the media, politicians, or captains of industry except when expedient for some short-term political gain. Those who do bring up the subject, regularly and seriously, are almost universally decried as anarchists.

That's not to say there is no connection between memes and the control virus; the Vyron is in fact a master manipulator of memes. Memes can be manufactured to carry the payload of the control virus into the culture. So in a sense, the virus often infects the mind first, or triggers the virus that might be lying dormant in a susceptible host. That brings me to an important point:

Any person, group, or belief system can be infected with the virus.

The virus does not belong to any party, religion, class or ideology, but rather adapts itself to any group or worldview that will help it spread. Once infected, these groups or ideologies become increasingly rigid, dogmatic, narrow, petty and ruthless, until they finally implode, leaving confusion and wreckage behind. Next I'll talk about how this happens.

Simplifying The Client I

I owe my initial understanding of the control virus to the great American prophet, William S. Burroughs. If humanity has evolved in any significant way since the time I am writing this then you will understand why I prefer the works of conspiracy theorists, pseudoscientists, and hallucinating drug addicts to tell my story. Throughout history they have been more reliable sources of truth and evolution than most of the professors, media pundits, and political operatives combined—all of whom are paid to obscure, in one way or another, the official record of a nation.

Burroughs understood the ways of the control virus better than most because he himself was infected with it for most of his life. He even committed the ultimate act of control, by killing his wife in a drunken game of William Tell.

Burroughs would go in and out of the Vyron's control for the rest of his life, haunted by guilt, ruined by drugs, and horrified by the ultimate control force ever invented, the atomic bomb. All the while he dogged the Vyron like a detective, following its destruction through the proxies of addiction, sex, language, government, family, and church. Near the end of his life Burroughs finally underwent an exorcism to fully rid himself of the Vyron, a kind of deathbed conversion common to virus-carriers who face the ultimate disinfectant: the bacteria that will claw and chew all of us into dust.

History has shown us repeatedly how easily powerful people, corporations, and even nations—managed and surrounded by the best and brightest—can fall into chaos, scandal, and ruin seemingly overnight. For this to happen, as we see so often in retrospect, a lot of people must make a number of very bad decisions without accurately assessing the consequences. I believe this process begins with infected persons in positions of power who in turn "simplify" those around and beneath them. Here is Burroughs, from *Naked Lunch*:

> The junk merchant doesn't sell his product to the consumer, he sells the consumer to his product. He does not improve and simplify his merchandise. He degrades and simplifies the client. (224)

Replace "junk" with "Vyron" and you have the business model of the control virus. The virus must simplify the healthy client before infection can occur. Therefore the Vyron is always to be found advocating expediency, raising alarms, and reducing complex human relationships to simplistic formulations of Us and Them.

To see how quickly the control virus can infect and overwhelm a segment of society, one can look at the rapid radicalization and self-destruction of the civil rights movement. Martin Luther King's assassination so traumatized the politically active youth in the nation that the movement itself was quickly infected and dominated by the virus. Opportunists filled the vacuum of leadership left by King's murder and began to turn into control addicts themselves, advocating violence, militarism, and even terror-ism to achieve their aims. I believe that this process was not a result of his assassination, but was in fact the *purpose* of it. The control addicts who murdered King did not do so because he fought for equal rights; they killed him because he did so peacefully.

Exposing people to violent trauma is not the only way to infect them with the control virus. Soon after the development of mass media it was discovered that people could be simplified by weaponizing words and phrases, sufficiently de-grading memes until they were hollowed out enough to carry a sufficient payload of the virus; that a sufficiently weaponized meme could in fact cause as much or more damage as any number of assassinations or wars.

One example of how weaponized memes can be deployed occurred within what was arguably the most successful and well-loved technology firm in its day, the Microsoft Corporation. After achieving astonishingly rapid success through its innovative software, and becoming arguably the most powerful technology company in history, the company took on a different, darker mission.

This mission, discovered in the company's internal memoranda during a court trial, was called "embrace, extend, extinguish." This was a policy whereby innovative new technologies were initially embraced by Microsoft, extended by attaching new software "hooks" to make the technology behave differently on Microsoft software and then, leveraging its near-monopoly in the operating systems market, extinguished when a nearly identical version of the software could be reverse-engineered by Microsoft programmers, at which point the "extended" version of the technology would be made incompatible, causing frustrated customers to abandon the innovative technology in favor of Microsoft's own (usually inferior) product.

While this policy reaped tremendous profits for Microsoft, far beyond even their earlier success, it also signaled that the Vyron had infiltrated the company at the highest levels. And although Microsoft is still tremendously profitable, and therefore able to enter and potentially dominate any market it chooses, the company's influence has steadily declined in recent years. At the time of this writing all its former innovative spirit is long gone, replaced by pure imitation, with less and less success. The company once known as an innovator and leader has been reduced to what could be described as corporate hysterics, jumping into video games, personal music players, Internet search and now retail stores as a direct response to successes by other companies that Microsoft has not been able to "extinguish".

Brutal strategies for defeating one's competitors are not limited to Microsoft, of course. But the corporate philosophy of embrace-extend-extinguish was a particularly stunning use of weaponized words being used to simplify the client (in this case, Microsoft employees and customers) in the service of the Vyron (the corporate leaders and mangers who initiated the policy).

This is only one example, but it is a good model for the methodology of the Vyron, which leverages wealth and power in order to simplify the client only because the true complexities and responsibilities of wealth and power are too difficult for it to understand.

What The Vyron Wants

If the desire to dominate and destroy others is the result of infection by the control virus, a contagious pathogen that causes changes in the neuroanatomy or even genetic makeup of the infected, such a discovery would not only be a tremendous medical breakthrough but would answer some of the most vexing moral and philosophical questions mankind has ever struggled with: What is evil? Why does it exist? And, Why is it so hard to get a live person on the telephone?

We still have very romantic notions of evil. We believe it is motivated by money, power, sex, or fame. This is incorrect. The Vyron derives no joy from these things; it is incapable of happiness, humor, love; it is never, ever satisfied. It desires money or power only because acquiring them enables it to fulfill its true destiny. The control virus wants only one thing, lives for one thing—the same thing that all viruses want, the only reason for its existence:

Replication.

That's it. That is the only goal of any virus, including the Vyron. The control virus seeks control over others *only to make others more susceptible to infection with the control virus.*

People with wealth and power who are not infected with the Vyron take all available measures to protect their wealth and power; the Vyron-controlled entity, however, winds up doing nothing but attempting to spread itself to others, and when it has succeeded, it promptly self-destructs.

America's Epitaph

I said the Vyron weaponizes words, prefera-
bly meaningless, easily understood phrases and
soundbites that simplify the client, facilitating
infection in the service of replication. Some of
the memes the Vyron has weaponized for this
purpose over the years include "Duck and
cover," "Just say no," "Drill baby drill," "Hope,"
and "Change." It is only when the weaponized
memes have taken strong enough effect, and op-
ponents to the adulterated memes have been
sufficiently weakened, that the virus can move on
to the second stage of its replication campaign:
physical domination.

This is an area that other writers, especially
Huxley and Orwell, have already covered thor-

oughly, but it's worth looking at again specifically with regards to what killed America.

Wherever the control virus holds sway, you see the paradox of ever more chaos regarding an increasingly dualistic, simplistic worldview. It would seem to follow that as one's worldview becomes simplified so would one's response mechanisms, but in the case of the Vyron the opposite occurs.

As the Vyron simplified the client—in this case, America—it became more and more strident, more Manichean, more fundamental, literal, rigid, dogmatic. The national body, having become infected with the Vyron, came to believe that tolerance and self-awareness were the problems. Whenever the desire for peace tried to spread, as it did after the disasters of the 1960s—the Bay of Pigs, political assassinations and Vietnam War—the virus became more miserable, angry, depressed. To placate the virus the government issued more and more policies of domestic violence, surveillance, and control against the people. In other words, it unleashed more of the Vyron against the control infection the protests were trying to cure. As I write this, roughly 40 years after Woodstock, pundits are still complaining that these few years of innocent rebellion, long hair, drug experimentation and romantic adventurism are to blame for every problem our nation has faced since. And I believe this long-festering grudge, this hatred the Vyron feels towards expressions of love, freedom, and peace, was the motivation for the most destructive word-weapon ever created.

The weaponized meme I am about to unveil has unleashed more of the control virus—and therefore more misery, death, waste, and abuse—over the past 15 years than any other in modern history. It is a meme that has taken various guises over the years, but was not officially weaponized in America until 1994 to my knowledge. I will introduce this phrase to you now, but I must warn you: it is so powerful that I must put it on its own page, so as to isolate the phrase and keep it away from the other words in this book as much as possible. As I type it I will be looking away from the screen, to reduce my exposure to the control virus via the atomized delivery device known as the pixel. You have been warned.

Zero Tolerance

There, I did it. Have you turned the page? Is it gone yet? Is it safe to look?

Oh, children of the future! If you have to put one epitaph on the tombstone of America, use those two words. Those words signaled our coming destruction. It was the most evil word-weapon ever used against its own people. You must understand that phrase if you are to understand how America died. Fear that phrase, but not so much that you inadvertently will it back into existence. Treat it as you would any other highly toxic substance, and please take the necessary precautions. If you possibly can then by all means destroy that phrase, burn it, shun it, for the sake of whatever you hold holy.

Once unleashed, the phrase exploded through our nation with shocking speed and force. It was used indiscriminately against young and old, the guilty and not guilty alike. It turned every citizen into a suspect overnight, instantly criminalized the entire population and claimed dominion over our every thought, action, and desire. It was the greatest single theft of our freedoms, morality, and humanity. It was joyfully invoked against schoolchildren as young as five who were arrested, handcuffed, and charged with sexual assault for touching other children on the schoolyard. It was invoked today, as I'm writing this, by the board of a Middle School in Connecticut, which has just banned any and all physical contact whatsoever between students. No hugs or handshakes, no pats on the back, no holding hands. *Zero Tolerance.* It has been invoked in Wyoming, where a prosecutor is charging three teenage girls with felony pornography charges for allowing their pictures to be taken while wearing their bras.

Of course, America has never been a place of actual tolerance; laws protecting certain so-called inalienable rights have occasionally pulled the snapping dogs from the throats of those foolish enough to exercise those rights, but they have never kept the fangs out of our necks in the first place. Our corporate media actors lectured us that we should be grateful that we had a mechanism for occasionally pulling the dogs from our throats, and that all we suffered from is ingratitude. They told us that we should be grateful for any moments of our lives that were not under assault by the dogs of Freedom. From this they came to the sad but inescapable conclusion that our method for removing the dogs from our throats—the judiciary—must be in fact the cause of our ingratitude, and therefore the dog-catching apparatus of equal protection and fair trials must be dismantled if we were to become more Free.

Why did seemingly sane people allow this to happen? Because the Vyron had been practicing, probing, testing us for weakness for some time, in plain sight. To condition the populace the word-weapon of "zero tolerance" was used first against outright criminals, then non-criminal drug "offenders" and those found "driving under the influence" of alcohol. Upon the success of these programs the Vyron expanded its campaign and targeted people who are not criminals at all, beginning with smokers, and rapidly expanded to include those who do not wear seatbelts, or helmets, or water wings. It has been tested out in New York against parents who refuse to put their children on mind-altering medications if the school demands it. Mayor Bloomberg threatened to take children away from any parents who did not comply with forced medication; for the time being he has backed off. But he, or a predecessor, will be back to finish the job. The Vyron always comes back. It always finishes the job

Now that these weakening agents have taken hold, the Vyron has recently been test-marketing its newest, most innovative control product:

Obeying the law is no excuse.

Tasers are an example of this. In late America police routinely shot citizens with thousands of volts of electricity, often resulting in death, without any justifiable reason. Once upon a time the phrase "unlicensed driver" meant driving without having been properly licensed by the state, or for driving after having had driving privileges previously revoked for some infraction. Now it has been taken over by the virus to mean *driving without the physical ID card on your person.* In fact in America it is now illegal to walk down the street without one's identification cards, or else one risks arrest and imprisonment without trial, at the pleasure of the police. This has been done in the name of security, under the guise of freedom; in reality it has been done solely for the pleasure and gratification of the control virus.

No interpretation of the law is too petty, limiting, or literal for the virus. That is why the virus always reverts to fundamentalism, literalism, invoking safety, expediency and decisiveness to justify its existence.

Just today, in the April 6, 2009 *Washington Post* came the news that a high school student faces expulsion for taking a legal, prescribed birth control pill. "Zero Tolerance" policies against drugs have led to banning aspirin, Tylenol, even cough drops and simple cold remedies in schools, under threat of expulsion. One enlightened school district, according to the *Post*, recently allowed students to carry cough drops, but *not to share them*. The case of a 13-year old Arizona student, who was strip-searched for suspicion of carrying ibuprofen, will soon be brought before the U.S. Supreme Court.

By focusing only on the alleged legality of the assault—and that's exactly what it was—the people involved can avoid the truth: that it was meant to humiliate the child as much as possible, and to inflict enough emotional distress to simplify the victim (a former A-student whose life was forever changed and seriously harmed as a result).

Even if the court does its work, and the student prevails, nothing will change. Slightly modified policies will be suggested, certain "safeguards" debated, while across the media the Vyron will rage that not being able to strip search, expel, and forever traumatize children will cause immeasurable harm to our nation. Simultaneously these virus-carriers will insist that they are motivated *solely by the children's best interests*. The more enlightened (or devious) will admit, occasionally, that perhaps mistakes have been made—just not in sufficient quantity or extremity to in any way cast blame upon those who committed the assault.[8] The gross psychological distortion that such policies cause—that certain people are assumed guilty until proven innocent while others are presumed innocent even once proven guilty—has led me to one inescapable conclusion:

---

[8] As I was preparing this book for publication the Supreme Court decided in favor of the teen (June 2009). In a very close and confusing decision the court found that the teen's rights had indeed been violated, but that the perpetrators *could not be held responsible*. The decision only underscored just how far removed we had become from notions of actual justice in late America: the court decided, essentially, that while zero tolerance was not sufficient justification for child molestation, it was not necessarily wrong.

Zero Tolerance is, *in all cases*, immoral, illegal, and insane.

At roughly the same time that some were threatening to snatch the children from parents who refused to give them potentially dangerous psychotropic drugs, as Mayor Bloomberg attempted to do in New York City, other children were being humiliated and traumatized for taking safe and legal, over-the-counter medications. This was not a contradiction; this was the Vyron working at its highest level. It was the criminalization of literally everything: compliance and non-compliance alike, simultaneously, in all directions at once. If you did not need medication you would be required to take it; if you *did* need medication you would be denied until you confessed, groveled, and submitted to the most profane invasions of your privacy, the endless examinations, inquisitions, and gropes of the morally depraved. Either way you would be *punished*.

A Manhattan mother, Lenore Skenazy, was recently dubbed "the worst mom in the world" because she let her articulate and intelligent 11-

year-old son ride the subway alone. A recent survey discovered that more than 40% of American children feel it is "very likely" that they will be abducted and/or killed. An 11-year old can see his mother vilified for allowing him to feel free and adventurous; those same parents demonizing her see nothing wrong with their own children living in terror of being kidnapped and mutilated.

Once unleashed upon the people, the malignant word-weapon of Zero Tolerance grew more powerful and pervasive, infecting the minds of liberals and conservatives alike, each of whom attached the phrase to their own spheres of influence in their own ways, so that by the end of America you could find the phrase underlying or outright dictating the policies of every school, office, church, stadium, restaurant, bar, bowling alley, airport, park and home in America.

Republicans and Democrats embraced the phrase, loved it, nurtured it, and worked tirelessly to find new applications for it. Zero Tolerance for jaywalking! Zero Tolerance for leaving the toilet seat up! Zero Tolerance for the mentally ill, perverts, drunks, druggies, teenagers, recreational sex, the confused, the lost, the lonely, the unemployed, the cheated, the elderly; Zero Tol-

erance for loud music, the expression of impure
thoughts, public displays of affection, nursing
mothers and peaceful protests. Zero Tolerance
for carrying lipstick, toothpaste, or emery boards
onto airplanes; Zero Tolerance for any signs of
joy, life, expression, or difference.

And that was only the virus carried in one
meme! Multiply that by the billions of memes in
the millions of memeplexes, and you can understand why the greatest destroyer of American
freedoms did not come from terrorists crossing
her borders but the memes of mass destruction
unleashed upon the trusting and unguarded
minds of its own citizens.

The second most powerful word-weapon was
the prefix "War On." The origins of it actually
preceded Zero Tolerance, but it took second
place because there were many more things to
have zero tolerance about than to declare war
on. Regardless, they complemented one other
and were often used to justify the other. War On
Terror, War On Drugs, War On Poverty, War
On Illiteracy; wars on teen pregnancy, drunk
driving, ingratitude—you name it there was a

War On it, backed by some leering agent of the Vyron claiming a constitutional and God-given right to ZERO TOLERANCE.

Such memes are perfect carriers for the virus because they are as stupid and simplistic as the virus itself. Complexity, redundancy, and tolerance breed resistance to the Vyron, which is why the real war going on at any time was the ongoing effort to simplify the client. Intolerance, rigidity, and the demand for expedience are the hallmarks of viral urgency: the virus does not find enough injection points in something that has strength through being flexible, communicative, responsive, giving or yielding. Ironically, though the control virus is ostensibly always looking for compliance and acquiescence, passive or otherwise malleable structures prove too resistant, so first the virus must somehow stiffen, paralyze, or disorient the chosen victim.

This is where our political distinctions fall apart, because these word-weapons have infected and taken over both sides with few exceptions, pushing any rational dissenters into the margins. Who would dare argue against zero tolerance for child molesters, drunk drivers, wife beaters, cop killers, terrorists? A sane country recognizes that the monsters who commit such acts must be punished in proportion to the crime, without succumbing to vengeance; a Vyron-controlled country uses these people to inure the populace to the ideas of Zero Tolerance that will then be turned against the law-abiding.

When faced with the malignant word-weapon of Zero Tolerance a rational person should respond, "A free and just society is completely incompatible with the concept of zero tolerance." That is where the virus, sensing itself about to be exposed, will respond with hysterics and outrage: "Soft on crime! Child molesters! Cop killer!" By narrowing the debate down to the warhead of a weaponized meme like "zero tolerance" the virus threatens the non-compliant with a calculated and pre-planned explosion of personal destruction and slander, threatening to destroy the reputations, livelihoods, and make social pariahs of those who do not buckle under.

There is a third word-weapon being used against us, and it is perhaps the most insidious and frightening of them all: The Children. The Vyron tyrannizes us with The Children, even while attempting to drive families further apart in order to infect the most vulnerable members of society. The sick relationship between the Vyron and "the children" is so complex that it would require its own book.[9]

---

[9] You are invited to submit your own thoughts or chapters about how the concept of "the children" is being used as a weapon against us. The best submissions will appear in future editions of this book. Please refer to the section "About The Living Book" at the end.

Simplifying The Client II

For a wicked and evil concept like Zero Tolerance to take hold, and then be used indiscriminately by people of all political, economic, and social levels, the control virus must first simplify the people into believing it is a valid concept. I believe one of the ways it does this is by first waging war against privacy at the smallest levels. Simplification begins not in the corridors of power, but at the back fences of America.

The Vyron is always snooping; most gossips are under the influence of the control virus to some degree. In popular culture these gossips take the form of entertainment media, including the paparazzi that stalk and terrorize those cursed with fame. In the epidemiology of the Vy-

ron the paparazzi don't sell pictures of the famous, they sell an image of the famous *being
terrorized*—weaponizing the image-meme just as
politicians weaponized "zero tolerance." We are
told that celebrities "ask for it," that they are
"fair game." According to reports published at
the time, when Princess Diana's driver was found
to have alcohol in his system, one of the professional gossips that dispatched the killer
motorcyclists breathed a *sigh of relief*. There would
be no day of reckoning for the Vyron.

I said that I am not political, but that is still
more of a goal than a reality. Although my de-
programming is almost complete I weaken; I
take sides; I look Left or Right instead of Straight
Ahead.

The fact is I do have political leanings, and
they fall squarely into the philosophy of the Order of the Anti-Poke-Noses, a society formed in
the 1920s to mock the Ku Klux Klan. The group
set as its noble goal, "To oppose any organiza-
tion that attends to everybody else's business but
their own."

Where are you now, my friends?

We are addicted to poking our noses into the
business of others. Another great American
prophet, H.L. Mencken, called the objects of

provincial gossip Yokels, the fresh meat upon
whom the nose pokers could sharpen their teeth:

> The yokel has scarcely any privacy at all. His
> neighbors know everything that is to be
> known about him, including what he eats and
> what he feeds his quadruped colleagues. His
> religious ideas are matters of public discus-
> sion; if he is recusant the village pastor prays
> for him by name. When his wife begins the
> biological process of giving him an heir, the
> news flies around. If he inherits $200 from
> an uncle in Idaho, everyone knows it in-
> stantly. If he skins his shin, or buys a new
> plow, or sees a ghost, or takes a bath it is a
> public event. Thus living like a goldfish in a
> glass globe, he acquires a large tolerance of
> snoutery, for if he resisted it his neighbors
> would set him down as an enemy of their
> happiness, and probably burn his barn. It
> seems natural and inevitable to him that eve-
> ryone outside his house should be interested
> in what goes on inside, and that this interest
> should be accompanied by definite notions
> as to what is nice and what is not nice, sup-
> ported by pressure. So he submits to
> government tyranny as he submits to the vil-
> lage inquisition, and when he hears that city

men resist, it only confirms his general feel-
ing that they are scoundrels. They are
scoundrels because they have a better time
than he has — the sempiternal human reason[10]

To accept loss of privacy, whether by government or family, friend or neighbor, is to cede
to the all-consuming mouth of *snoutery*.

Mencken's Yokel is not very different from
what Burroughs might have called the simplified
client. Both are under complete control of outside forces; both are stripped of their privacy and
therefore dignity. The retail version of the Vyron
is traded over every fence, in every barbershop
and every bible study meeting, doled out one
morsel of gossip at a time.

Put up a No Smoking sign and the conservative is annoyed while the liberal is pleased. Put
up a No Talking sign and the liberal is annoyed
but the conservative is pleased. Put up a sign that
says Mind Your Own Business and they will both
erupt in rage.

---

[10] From *A Second Mencken Chrestomathy*, retrieved from
http://www.sadlyno.com/archives/date/2007/11/page/3

Media, Artists, and the Vyron

America's Founders, in their great wisdom, understood the control virus very well, which was why they went to such great lengths to develop the most advanced warning and deterrent systems yet devised by man: freedom of speech, and a free and adversarial press. To understand how America died we must therefore take a look at why and how these systems failed.

The media, seeing its power grow exponentially through radio and television, began to manufacture the news based on its own image, in active collusion with the government powers and business interests that flanked it. Journalists ceased being reporters in any meaningful sense and became entertainment personalities, increasingly drawn from the same small pool of elite universities, think tanks, and lobbying groups of the industry leaders and politicians they were supposed to be covering. Over time, the media came to assume that it was speaking for the nation when it spoke on behalf of increasingly narrow interests. When occasionally challenged on their bias—such as happened in the early years of the Internet Age, when citizens began fighting back against this corruption—the media concocted elaborate denials absolving themselves or, when that failed, pushed the idea that "we all" were responsible.

This slow and suffocating change took place over decades, but greatly accelerated during America's final years. When information that was never meant to be made public surfaced— the Zapruder film, for example, or the details surrounding Watergate—the effect upon the people was so powerful that the political elites redoubled their efforts to control the news industry, although in increasingly sophisticated and covert ways. Frightened by the power of the democracy they claimed to love, they unleashed private industry to do their dirty work instead. They began by eroding ownership rules, in the name of "free markets," which allowed huge financial trusts and global corporations to monopolize, alienate, and then snuff out the functional press in favor of its own grotesque simulation. This was a task for which the trusts were particularly well suited, having carried out similar takeovers in many other industries over the years: mortgaging the companies' assets while falsely inflating their values and simultaneously draining the (temporarily-increased) profits. Once the cycle became unsustainable the trusts then slashed the core businesses until quality, morale, and customers declined sufficiently so that bankruptcy became inevitable and the mess was foisted back upon the American people to clean up at their expense. At this point the trusts would go back to the government for further regulations, handouts, and expanded power, to protect themselves from the consequences of their own misdeeds.

By the time we realized that the goals of modern finance and a free society were entirely incompatible and in fact antagonistic, it was too late.

To counter the trend that they themselves created (or to mask and even accelerate it, if you're conspiratorial by nature), the financial trusts hired new classes of entertainers to give the appearance of engagement, passion, and spontaneity in the news while ensuring that the message became even more tightly focused on the best interests of the financial trusts.

These actors took several forms, which were actually variations on the same model: the reactionary extremist.

The first variation called themselves "conservatives." The job of these actors was to simplify viewers and listeners by preaching a non-stop gospel of intolerance, war, and profligacy. They filled the airwaves with sobs and screams about how the decline of America could be directly traced to insufficient obedience to authority and lack of respect for corporate morality. Day and night, to millions of viewers and listeners on national television and radio, they cried that their voices were being stifled by a powerful evil conspiracy known as "the liberal media."

Reactionary extremists were for the most part white males, and included Bill O'Reilly, Rush Limbaugh, Michael Gerson, Glenn Beck and Ann Coulter.

To balance this cult of corporate victimology, so-called "moderate" voices were elevated alongside the conservatives. These moderates, or "centrists"—despite their self-proclaimed love of balance and reason—nevertheless found themselves gently coming to the defense of the conservatives with near 100% certainty, but did so in nuanced, greasy, pseudo-rational tones.

These passive-aggressive preachers spoke of the unfortunate *necessity* of torture and war; maintained earnestly that whatever mistakes were made, America was still and always would be a *great country*; urged that we obey and believe with all our hearts and minds the reactionary extremists, no matter what the outcome. They celebrated the cult of American mediocrity and obsessed over the imagined needs "regular folks," while supporting the most radical, reactionary, and brutal practices of late American regimes.

These closet extremists were usually white females, and had names like Diane Sawyer, Maureen O'Dowd, Cokie Roberts, Peggy Noonan, and David Brooks.

Therefore the role of the reactionary extremists posing as moderates was to legitimize the reactionary extremists posing as conservatives, by smoothing over their words and gently driving

home the point that the conservative, while perhaps a bit hotheaded and passionate, was
ultimately *correct*. They played the role of ena-
bling mommy to angry daddy.

But this was not enough. By the end of
America consumers were not entirely ignorant of
the crudities of information marketing, and a
majority began expressing extreme skepticism
against the corporate media. Ever adaptive, and
with nearly infinite resources at their collective
disposal, the financial trusts created a third class
of media performer to give the appearance of
balance. These were the contrarians, and they
were arguably the worst of all.

The contrarians, as their name obviously im-
plies, was just another form of reactionary
extremist, but with a twist. The role of the contrarian was to add some spice to the mommy-
daddy debate of the conservatives and moderates. Like the fiesty child in a television sitcom,
the contrarian cocked his cap sideways and came
onto the set with a slingshot in the pocket of his
cuffed dungarees, making mommy and daddy
forget their surface disagreements and come together in a big scene-ending hug.

There were of course no real differences
among the contrarian, conservative, and moder-

ate except tone and emphasis. The conservative hid his love of control behind vague talk of "values" and nostalgia for a non-existent golden age; the moderate believed we could all learn to love the control virus by using *nicer language.*

The contrarian, on the other hand, openly celebrated his intoxication with the Vyron. He spent his time looking for emerging power trends and then, once he believed he had found a winner, loudly signaled the new infection target by proclaiming his devotion to it, noisily dismissing his previous object of worship as somehow outdated, foolish. The contrarian was, like his teen counterpart on television, the ultimate consumer, obsessed with trends and fads and always agitating for some new control product to be brought into the national family. The contrarian was to power what the fashion magazines were to clothes, forever trumpeting a new hemline or heel as deeply meaningful and important.

This enabled the contrarian to bond with these new control products as they came to market, and allowed him to defend his choices with all the impetuous certainty of an adolescent. He debated the benefits of new control models with the conservative and moderate, who would argue in their own quaint, old-fashioned ways that the old control was fine, it just needed some sprucing up. The contrarian's job was to sell them on the attractive style, benefits and savings the new control system would confer.

This process of discarding cherished beliefs as soon as a new and improved one came along frequently created the appearance of hypocrisy in the contrarian, which the contrarian subsumed as a part of his personal mythology, proof of his divine incorruptibility and intellectual superiority. Everything in the contrarian's topsy-turvy world was always only evidence of an even *greater* integrity.

This cult of miraculous, spontaneous self-evolution was very difficult to pull off and therefore highly prized by the corporate media. It required a certain ruthless *hauteur* and inbred snobbery that most Americans simply lacked; therefore the most successful contrarians of our day, like Andrew Sullivan and Christopher Hitchens, were English.

As of this writing the media has begun test-marketing a new television product, the "non-reactionary." This is an extremely risky gambit, as it threatens to expose the fact that television media has, until now, been almost exclusively controlled by the three flavors of reactionary extremism; understandably, there has been tremendous outcry against these efforts.

It's too early to tell whether or not these new products will have any lasting unintended consequences against the control virus, or if they will be subsumed more completely into the control structure over time. The only two such test products, Keith Olbermann and Rachel Maddow, have not been on the air long enough, though initial ratings seem to be good. I personally believe that they do not yet represent a new class of pundit so much as a curious anomaly, which will be corrected within the next one or two election cycles lest they accidentally exert unwarranted influence on the populace.

The next class of watchdog to fail was the artist. Those who in the past could occasionally be counted upon to act as a kind of conscience for the media instead began to emulate them, herded into the same trap of corporate careerism that had caught the journalists and editors.

For an artist to exhibit a political passion or social conscience at the end of the 20th century was, with few exceptions, considered the height of bad taste. To do so was to risk ridicule from one's peers; the single greatest fear my fellow artists felt was that they might be considered *uncool.* This was the blackest mark for a hipster in late America, and those who didn't obey, and tried speaking out against injustice or cruelties, were openly mocked[11] or told to "just shut up."[12]

Perhaps the best evidence for this peer-imposed censorship can be found in the literary fiction of late America. As publishers were bought by the same trusts that owned the mass media, in the name of "synergy," mainstream literary fiction increasingly refused to concern itself in any serious way with socio-political issues for fear of offending those trusts. Authors put the fragile beauty of their sentences and the picayune observations of sensitive characters over all else. The supposedly big, important novels of our times were mostly mawkish, maudlin affairs: family dramas, dead children, substance abuse

---

[11] "[T]hese people are "Polits"—a combination of political activists and would-be literary types."— http://www.hipsterhandbook.com/ Quoted in http://gawker.com/011166/underground-literary-alliance
[12] http://www.thestranger.com/seattle/just-shut-up/Content?oid=13429

and shopping. These artists of course shared the same fears and opinions about the direction the country was going, but they were almost entirely silent about these concerns in their own work.

Remember that I am referring only to creative writers, and not those political and non-fiction writers who worked hard to expose truths about our society as best they could. I'm only concerned here with the novelists and short story writers who had seemingly abandoned the notion that they had any voice in the direction of the country, while simultaneously becoming this country's biggest educational product: two phenomena that I believe were connected.

The goal of literary fiction at the end of America was therefore reduced to little more than discussions of identity politics. This was not the fault of the writers, who were only trying to sell their manuscripts for the most part, but came from the publishing houses themselves. Just as identity politics had been elevated over any other considerations by late America, so too was social or political consciousness outside the realms of gender, ethnicity, or sexual preference considered passé in creative writing—even ridiculous.

This was not limited to literary fiction, but to the culture as a whole. The Gen-X, or "slacker" hipster of late America had been programmed to "drop out" of society, while adopting a kind of meek, eclectic consumerism—beginning in the early-to-mid 1980s—that celebrated ad hoc identities created from the detritus of childhood: thrift shop clothing, salvaged furniture, ironic artwork and dissonant music recorded on deliberately substandard equipment, for example.

Having debased themselves to visual analogs of poverty entirely removed from their own (primarily) comfortable middle-class existences, these late Americans evolved their aesthetic into an appreciation for foreign cultures that were even more destitute, leading to a rise of consumption of imported cultures and cuisines, while they themselves tended to move onto advanced degrees through the university system, thus entering the final stages of global sincerity-consumption. One example of this was the rise of "ecotourism," where the more esthetically thoughtful destruction of natural habitats was taken as a sign of great sophistication.

By the end of the 20th century the most popular of the luxury education products was the Masters of Fine Arts, or MFA program. The shabby chic of the 1980s "punk" and early-90s "grunge" years transitioned into a more well-groomed, well-spoken, but still utterly inert and disengaged class of corporate artist: those who pursued higher education because they believed wholeheartedly that art was a business that could only be learned, networked, and referenced into on the corporate-university level.

This elevation of the advanced university education to a pre-requisite for literary expression had its roots in the Cold War, when the CIA infiltrated many of the nation's cultural institutions, mostly famously the *Paris Review* (which it not only infiltrated but created). Since these early operatives were drawn from the elite worlds of Ivy League schools, global conglomerates and finance, America's literary life quickly became wedded to and indistinguishable from these interests. Rather than speaking truth to power the literary world began gossiping about itself, spying on itself. It is no surprise that the children of these gossips created a literature that was hopelessly confessional and exhibitionistic.

The brief rise of the Beat Generation was largely a reaction to this spreading influence (though the members were products of the same system, it should be noted). It is no surprise that they were attacked by the leading reactionary extremists of their day, like Norman Podhoretz, and Henry Luce's Time-Life empire.

Even as its sentences and situations became more elaborate, the range of allowable literary expression actually became narrower after the Cold War. Over the past 15 years I have attended dozens of readings and witnessed hundreds of authors reading their creative writing. It is no exaggeration to say that at least three-quarters of those writers have read personal, sentimental stories about their childhood. The remaining were a mix of poetry, genre, or experimental. No more than a handful read anything that could be remotely considered socially conscious, and not one made a single mention—apart from the usual stabs at American consumerism and "shallowness"—of our national soul or deeper values, the horrors being inflicted in our names around the globe, our secret torture programs, financial terrorists, media and political extremists. And that includes myself.

I sense that at some time soon corporate publishers and writing programs will allow discussion of more pressing subjects within literary fiction, in a language and style suitable to our times, but it will done in response to market opportunity; in other words, only when it can be reasonably assumed to be too late to do any good.

If it ever dawned on my fellow writers—my friends, peers and colleagues—that they were caught in a spiritual dead end, circling endlessly around a literary cul-de-sac that had been built, paved, and leased to them by the same financial trusts that ran the rest of the country then I never saw any evidence of it, or heard any protests from the writers themselves. To do so, I assume, would have been considered *uncool*.

Because the entire chain of production and distribution in the literary world was likewise controlled by a handful of corporations, in many cases the same trusts that owned the media, authors had learned that they could not be published unless they coordinated their visions with those of the corporate publishers. This was a role the writing schools were only too glad to fill, by grooming out every impurity of thought, inconsistency of syntax, or otherwise market-unfriendly tic in students' writing. In this way the publishers, who would have just as soon written the books themselves, could maintain a sense of detached pragmatism about what could or couldn't sell in the market. They could not write the books, so they wrote the authors instead.

I am not against personal stories or higher education at all, and salute those who are hungry for self-improvement; I'm both a writer of personal narratives and a student myself. But it is hard to see the rise of higher education alongside the complacency of my generation and not wonder about a connection.

The recent revelation, after years of whispers and denials, that the *Paris Review* had indeed been founded and funded by the CIA, and that George Plimpton and Peter Matthiessen were in fact spies for the government, was therefore greeted with theatrical yawns, eye rolls, or angry dismissals by those writers who had come to count on the *Paris Review* as an important career-building step.

This mindset was so deeply ingrained in the literary world that even in those rare instances when an individual from within the industry noticed that something was terribly wrong with our literary fiction, the results were sometimes unintentionally revealing.

A few years ago Laura Miller, an editor for the online magazine Salon.com, wrote an essay for the *New York Times Book Review* in which she wondered, "Where are all the novels about working?"[13] Ms. Miller seemed surprised that she did not know of any fictional works that used the workplace as a setting.

It was a stunning admission: in fact there were many engaging novels about work and the working life; the problem, which Miller did not seem able to grasp, was that these novels were not to be found in the catalogs of the major publishers. The people writing novels about work were those who had been specifically and categorically excluded from corporate publishing, and therefore did not exist.

It was a fascinating premise for an essay, and I wished Ms. Miller had followed the thought to its logical conclusion (i.e., where are all the novels about working *among the catalogs of the major literary publishers*); unfortunately, it didn't seem to occur to Miller that she was operating in a world where work and workers were despised by those who

---

[13] "Works For Me," *NY Times* 8/4/04.
http://www.nytimes.com/2004/08/08/books/review/08MILLERL.html

financed those very presses—that, having lived
her entire life within the bubble of literary man-
agement as defined by the corporate trusts, her
entire professional life had been carefully constructed for her around the exclusion of a
significant segment of the population, not because of merit but because of *perceived corporate
value*. Artistic works about workers, safety, exploitation, economic terrorism and the like had long
ago been deemed *uncool*, and therefore erased
from the official literary record of our times.

Alas, Miller stopped her thinking short,
quickly adding that she was only talking about
"good" novels. The meaning was clear: she was
talking about only those novels written by the
products of the best schools, and therefore those
least likely to have actually worked in any meaningful way, for any meaningful length of time, at
anything other than the kind of media or academic careers to which graduates usually aspire.
Miller then narrowed down her definition of
"working":

> If the office (or factory or restaurant) is
> where people find adventure, camaraderie,
> meaning and even intimacy, then it seems a

fine place to look for the novel's next great
motor.

Perhaps there's nothing dismissive about
those parentheses; perhaps Miller knows that the
people capable of producing a "good" novel are
those least likely to have worked in restaurants or
factories. It is funny that she should then refer to
the novel's next great motor, using the image of a
machine to drive...what, exactly? Ideas? Reader-
ship? Profits?

Those are all noble goals, but what Miller is
saying, whether she realizes it or not, is that not
only must the working life be co-opted as a
growth market for literature, but that it can *only
be done by those who are least likely to have work experience*. A simulated literature, created in a
laboratory like so many Frankenbooks, written in
florid detail by the ambitious products of a Luxury Consumer Education Complex that had
been created for just that purpose.

Miller's essay had the desired effect: a few
years later there was indeed a sudden rush of
books onto the market by those very students she
had exhorted: novels of bored, educated men
and women in cubicles who spent their fictional

lives wondering what they were doing in an office when they could be off, say, writing a novel about being in an office instead. These novels were entertaining enough, but none gave us a single new insight about the workplace, or gave us a glimpse of any life other than that of the typical clever young academic/media corporatist. They all had impeccable spelling and fashionable grammar and drew from the menu of pre-approved literary devices. In other words, according to Miller they were *good*.

It wasn't only the well-educated, either: writers of all backgrounds, having been cut off from the source of their own creative identities (i.e., having become more concerned with creating a marketable corporate persona than following any inner vision or conscience) became ever more outlandish and hysterical about tailoring themselves and their products for the corporations. Fake memoirs became common. One of the most celebrated young writers of our times, J.T. Leroy, *did not exist*—and it took nearly a decade for the deception to be uncovered. Writers from the most typical backgrounds refashioned themselves as lurid, damaged products of the streets. Every writer became a Holocaust Of One.

Poetry, as a result of the Beat writers as well as the general apathy of the reading public, resisted the trend towards simulation and commoditization, becoming instead a dreary academic career track, until it was reinvigorated by the tremendous profit potential of hip-hop culture, at which point it was turned into something called "spoken word" (and I defy you to find a more efficient, and nakedly corporate, descriptor than that).

A primary reason why the literary gatekeepers told anybody with a social conscience to "shut up" was because they themselves were maneuvering themselves to take credit for social consciousness, if and whenever it should become "hot" again. This desperate pre-positioning for possible future legitimacy was due at least in part to the fact that people of all artistic disciplines had become obsessed with a strange identitarian concept known as *authenticity*. Corporate control over our culture was so complete that by the end of America artists began to believe that authenticity was something detached from them, a scarce commodity that had to be fiercely competed for.

The desperate need for authenticity by these credentialed literary meritocrats was so overwhelming that an ambitious editor for the incredibly elite and powerful *New Yorker* magazine could refer to his work as "underground" without a trace of irony, and nobody in the literary world would dare laugh at him.

Some struggled against the tide, of course. There were warnings against this inherent falseness in late American life—Isidore Isou, Guy Debord, Philip K. Dick, Christopher Lasch and Marshall McLuhan, to name a few—but they were so overwhelmed by the momentum of history that it hardly mattered. Lasch's culture of narcissism or Debord's spectacular society were no longer things to be on guard against: the mirror, the simulation itself had become just as hotly desired by those very same artists and hipsters who had the most to lose by its adoption.

The failure of our media and cultural institutions did not come about not by the lack of good intentions or sincerity of the workers, but from indirect exposure to the control virus at the corporate level. As conglomerates accumulated, proscribed, leveraged, and then drained our most important institutions of their legitimacy and value—before discarding them—our nation grew progressively sicker. It was able to do this because the control virus had already tainted the money supply at every level, so much so that you children of the future will perhaps discover one day that the virus is still alive and active on the bills themselves—giving new meaning to the idea of money being the root of all evil.

Gaming The Corporative

To understand why our cultural defenses against the control virus failed, we must first understand how those defenses were connected to our society, and how they became vulnerable.

You might have heard that America had something called a "capitalist" economy, one that was forever at war with "socialist" or "communist" societies. This is more of the Vyron's client-simplification routine. America did not have a capitalist society, but another system altogether:

Corporatism.

Corporatism is not "rule by the corporation," though there is no doubt corporations wielded tremendous power in America. It is instead a political and economic system organized around the "corporative," or self-identifying group:

> The word "corporatism" is derived from the Latin word for body, corpus. This meaning was not connected with the specific notion of a business corporation, but rather a general reference to anything collected as a body. Its usage reflects medieval European concepts of a whole society in which the various components – e.g., guilds, universities, monasteries, the various estates, etc. – each play a part in the life of the society, just as the various parts of the body serve specific roles in the life of a body. [14]

Corporatism is essentially a kind of economic identity politics, just as identitarian concerns are an overt form of corporatism. A person might belong to many corporatives, just as a meme might belong to numerous memeplexes. Using my earlier analogy, the meme "Mars" might belong to the memeplexes of astrology, astronomy, planets, war and candy bars, for example. Like-

---

[14] http://en.wikipedia.org/wiki/Corporatism

wise, a politically active, Irish-American nurse might belong to the corporatives of "Democratic voter," "Irish," "nurse" and perhaps "union member," among others.

A corporatist state is rigidly hierarchal, and therefore highly susceptible to infection from the control virus. It was inconceivable by late America that the state should respect individual rights; liberals openly despised and mocked the idea, and conservatives believed that only wealthy white males or those within the "conservative" corporative deserved them. The war of "left" and "right" became one of abolishing individual rights versus privatizing them. The left transferred its concept of rights onto the ethnic or gender corporatives, promoting "multiculturalism" and "diversity," as the right transferred its hatred of the Other onto cynical proxies like "tax cuts" and "family values."

Both corporatives repeatedly went to the same arbiter to settle its disputes: the state. Over time this further legitimized the concept that not only our freedoms but also the validity of our identities were in fact *functions of the state*, to be decided by and granted to us by our central government.

As corporatives subsumed our identities and fed them back to the state in the form of perpetual grievance and struggle, our judicial system came under increasing attack by the corporatist state, with politicians threatening "activist" judges who "legislate" from the bench—increasingly strident warnings not to meddle in the monopoly of state control.

This is the system that had corrupted our newsgathering and cultural values, because as financial trusts gained control of these areas then the nature of the corporatives shifted as well—usually without most of the participants being aware of the shift. Using my earlier example of Microsoft, by the time the company decided to "embrace, extend, extinguish" its competitors—once it took on the dualistic thinking of the control virus—it ceased being part of the software, technology, and computer corporatives and became something apart and isolated: a *Microsoft* corporative, unmoored from its own history and therefore doomed to fail in its future endeavors.

The identity crisis of modern literature can be traced to the same profound corporative shift, as publishers stopped being part of the "book publishing" corporative and became part of the "global media conglomerate" and "publicly-traded corporation" corporatives. This shift created some fundamental changes: first, there was a need to streamline and accelerate the production process. To make the process more efficient and profitable new barriers to entry were constructed, through middlemen and trade schools. The agent stood between author and publisher, and became a formidable barrier; eventually many agents themselves would not consider looking at the work of authors, but would only consider recommendations from their current authors. As the barriers to entry grew higher would-be authors flocked to the universities, who promised to give aspiring writers the tools, and even the connections, to get inside the publishing corporative. Faced with the rising flood waters of the shifting corporative, writers scrambled to not be left behind, running up the academic pyramids constructed for them, essentially, by the global publishing conglomerate and literary agent corporatives.

This was how the act of literature came to mimic the financial corporatives that owned the publishers: authors were increasingly told that in order to succeed they needed what was essentially an advanced business degree for the act of writing: the marketing was so successful that by 2002 the number of MFAs being awarded surpassed the number of MBAs for the first time in history. Our "literary fiction" showed the results of this shift, and much of it had all the surprise, warmth or humanity of a stock chart.

Likewise, a newspaper like the *New York Times* went bankrupt because, once it diversified into owning sports teams and real estate, it was no longer part of the "newspaper" corporative. The journalist corporative likewise followed, and made as its first priority to not offend those in power, because to do so would have been to lose access to them. It was inconceivable to the members of such a media corporative that they had an individual right and moral obligation to access elected officials; to the media corporative, to insult the political corporative would be to embarrass the journalist corporative, which nobody was willing to do. That was why, at the end of America, we had the least adversarial, most complacent and smug, essentially worthless news industry in our nation's history, a laughingstock across much of the world.

I do not know enough about the history of Hollywood to assess whether or not it has fallen to a model of pure corporatism, or if it was ever different. Perhaps its geographic distance from the media, literary, and financial nexus of New York has allowed it to develop differently; perhaps not.

An excellent introduction to corporatism can be found an in essay by libertarian writer Anthony Gregory, "Corporatism and Socialism in America":

> Principled advocacy of the free market requires an understanding of the differences between genuine free enterprise and "state capitalism." Although the Left frequently exaggerates and overemphasizes the evils of corporate America, proponents of the free market often find themselves in the awkward position of defending the status quo of state capitalism, which is in fact a common adversary of the free marketer and the anti-corporate leftist....
>
> Indeed, corporatism, implemented by the state — whether through direct handouts, corporate bailouts, eminent domain, licensing laws, antitrust regulations, or environmental edicts — inflicts great harm

on the modern American economy. Although leftists often misunderstand the fundamental problem plaguing the economy, they at least recognize its symptoms.

Conservatives and many libertarians, on the other hand, frequently dismiss many ills such as poverty as fabricated by the left-liberal imagination, when in fact it does a disservice to the cause of liberty and free markets to defend the current system and ignore very real and serious problems, which are often caused by government intervention in the economy. We should recognize that state corporatism is a form of socialism, and it is nearly inevitable in a mixed economy that the introduction of more socialism will cartelize industry and consolidate wealth in the hands of the few.

Leftists usually understand how wartime provides politically connected corporations with high profits and cushy contracts. What is more often neglected is that the history of the American domestic welfare and regula-

tory state also corresponds closely to the
rise of corporatism. It is no coincidence."[15]

I highlight this passage not as an endorse-
ment of Mr. Gregory's political views but
because it reveals an important fact about
American society at the end: our political argu-
ments rarely strayed beyond the realm of which
corporatives should be given preferential treat-
ment by the state. None was engaged in any
meaningful way—apart from the occasional free-
thinker like Mr. Gregory—with the issue of
whether or nor corporatism *itself* was the problem, or what to do about it.

What was the result of all this bickering
among corporatives? Over the last century, regardless of party, public sentiment, political
posturing or media manipulation, no matter
which party has been in power, there has been
only one constant:

**State control over our lives
has *always* increased.**

[15] http://www.lewrockwell.com/gregory/gregory64.html

Steadily, constantly, irrevocably. Whether small-government conservative or Big Brother liberal, we not only ceded total power to the state but, having run out of things to give it control of, began inventing new things (like strip-searching children on suspicion of carrying aspirin, for example). We had become inured to it, expecting a little bit more of our freedom to be taken away year after year to the point that we no longer cared when the increasingly rare impediment—usually brought by "crazy idealists" like the ACLU or occasional filibuster—caused a minor delay. Democrats led us into two ruinous world wars, Vietnam, and dropped the atomic bomb, yet liberals accused Republicans of being war-mongers; conservatives accused Democrats of overspending in the service of a totalitarian nanny-state while Republicans sold the country into debt slavery and engaged in endless culture wars at home.

Behind this bickering, and according to the true corporative to which they belonged—the *political power* corporative—both parties worked together to increase its own power at the expense of the citizens.

Woodrow Wilson advocated spreading capitalism backed by force every bit as passionately as George W. Bush would nearly a century later;[16] The neo-conservative William F. Buckley Jr. railed against the evil of labor unions but pledged fealty to the military-industrial complex[17]; self-proclaimed individualist Ayn Rand believed that individual rights were valid only when given by the state, and that human beings whose governments did not grant them individual rights could and should be murdered without remorse.[18]

---

[16] "Since trade ignores national boundaries and the manufacturer insists on having the world as a market, the flag of his nation must follow him, and the doors of the nations which are closed must be battered down...Concessions obtained by financiers must be safeguarded by ministers of state, even if the sovereignty of unwilling nations be outraged in the process. Colonies must be obtained or planted, in order that no useful corner of the world may be overlooked or left unused"—1907 speech, excerpted in *The Tragedy Of American Diplomacy*

[17] "...we have got to accept Big Government for the duration -- for neither an offensive nor a defensive war can be waged, given our present government skills, except through the instrument of a totalitarian bureaucracy within our shores..." *Commonweal*, 1952

[18] It's wrong to attack a country that respects (or even tries to respect) individual rights. If you do, you're an aggressor and are morally wrong. But if a "country" does not protect rights--if a group of tribesmen are the slaves of their tribal chief--why should you respect the "rights" that they don't have or respect? *Ayn Rand Answers*, p. 102-104

By the end of America the only real socio-economic debate at any given time was over what kind of state control each side preferred.

Conspiracies & The Vyron

This is the greatest thing in history!

-President Harry S Truman, upon learning that
the first atomic bomb had been dropped on Hiroshima

A control addict is never after control for the sake of it. That's only the first step. Once it has control the virus becomes increasingly restless and miserable until it can find an outlet for itself, a way to infect others. The long buildup of tensions between nations that inexorably explode in war are the foreplay of the virus, as it performs a slow and complex frottage against possible partners—probing for weakness, provoking responses, raising and lowering tensions as necessary—that will eventually allow it to detonate once again across the world.

Politics has always been a favorite profession for the Vyron. Besides granting a great deal of power, which the Vyron needs, more than any other job politics requires deception, dualism, demonization—the only activities at which the Vyron truly excels. Politicians are exposed to the most vulnerable sides of people, and are therefore presented with a rich and neverending buffet of infection-ripe targets.

Eventually this temptation was too great for American politicians, who turned against the people in full force, via a neverending spiral of taxes, wars, and petty legislations designed to drive the ordinary citizen crazy with paranoia, guilt, and harassment. Zero Tolerance was the only law of the land at the end of America; if a politician were to suggest that the business of governance should perhaps be more concerned with America's financial ruin than with whether children should be arrested for not wearing bicycle helmets, he or she would have been laughed out of the capitol.

Throughout history the Vyron has mocked any attempts to identify, isolate, and name the control virus as nothing more than conspiracy theories. And yet the Vyron itself is forever claiming to be under assault by vast and nameless conspiracies, which are usually nothing more than the reports and reverberations of its own actions upon the world. Hating weakness, the Vyron claims to be helpless as a kitten; despising compassion, the Vyron will claim that any thwarted acts of sadism are proof that it is simply "too nice"; hating freedom, the Vyron will legislate a world of zero tolerance for others and zero accountability for itself, while turning the screws ever tighter on the poor, the weak, the vulnerable. Hating sex, children, family and community, the Vyron will claim to stand, defend, and speak for these values above all.

To understand just how powerful and destructive the Vyron had become in our political system, one can look back to the period between the dropping of the first atomic bomb in Hiroshima and the political assassination of John F. Kennedy. These twin horrors were the bookends of nearly two decades of almost surreal depravity and brutality in American life, when everything we had ostensibly stood for as a nation was finally overthrown and replaced with its false or Vyron equivalent.

To understand how the Vyron gained control of our country during those years would take more time and talent than I possess, but if you are interested then you would do worse than to look at the personal histories of two of the most powerful men during the era, J. Edgar Hoover and Lyndon B. Johnson. Both were paranoid, bullying megalomaniacs who were as obsessed with digging up dirt on others as they were with keeping their own unsavory secrets hidden. Both were lifelong devotees of the control virus, dedicated to dominating and destroying others through murder, blackmail, plots, and assassinations. Both were among the worst monsters in American history.

I do not bring up these men to rehash their many crimes, all of which have been detailed elsewhere; the point is that these two men best represent the psyche of the Vyron as it applied to late America. Even after the posthumous revelations that Hoover and Johnson were malevolent, lawbreaking monsters who committed many crimes to gain and then maintain power, the official record of America, like Hoover's decades-long denial of the mafia, continued to deny even the *possibility* that a criminal conspiracy could exist within the halls of power in Washington.

The fact that America was the victim of a terrorist conspiracy on September 11, 2001 is accepted as simple truth, yet to suggest that the massive stock market transactions that occurred the day before, in those stocks directly affected by the attacks, and which trades were executed by a firm (Alex. Brown) whose previous chairman had by then become the number three man at the CIA—essentially proving prior knowledge of the attacks—is considered crazy by the official record. (The *9/11 Commission Report* sidestepped the issue by claiming that the firm "could not possibly have any ties to Al-Qaeda"—a strange conclusion, since foreknowledge of the attacks obviously would not require any "ties" to the attackers, only access to high-level intelligence.)

To the control virus, conspiracy theories are valid only if they further the aims of the Vyron, in its drive to cast itself as history's one true victim. In the world of the Vyron the only valid conspiracies are those of the weak against the powerful; poor against wealthy; the few solitary, honest observers against the secretive forces who have the power to monitor, spy, and kill with impunity. To believe in any other conspiracies was considered crazy.

The Way Forward

In order to get a sense of where the Vyron might be heading next I want to first jump back 160 years, to the words of another discredited and despised pseudoscientist, Karl Marx:

> The productive forces at the disposal of society no longer tend to further the development of the conditions of bourgeois property; on the contrary, they have become too powerful for these conditions, by which they are fettered, and so soon as they overcome these fetters, they bring disorder into the whole of bourgeois society, endanger the existence of bourgeois property. The conditions of bourgeois society are too narrow to comprise the wealth created by them. And how does the bourgeoisie get over these cri-

ses? On the one hand, **by enforced destruction of a mass of productive forces**; on the other, by the conquest of new markets, and by the more thorough exploitation of the old ones. That is to say, **by paving the way for more extensive and more destructive crises, and by diminishing the means whereby crises are prevented.**[19]

I use this quote from Marx not out of any political sympathy or kinship. His ideas are, to this writer, a blueprint for a different, but no less horrific system of control. Still, the above quote is very useful when examining the global economic chaos of the past several decades. There has indeed been an unbroken string of global financial crises, precisely this "enforced destruction of a mass of productive forces" brought about through determined and malicious financial engineering and terrorism—huge convulsions in Russia, Argentina, Asia, Iceland and Eastern Europe, to name just a few.

In the past two decades the United States has succumbed to the poison of the financial Vyron,

---

[19] *Communist Manifesto*, 1848

and gone through a series of massive stock, debt and real estate bubbles. America had reached the point where the financial deception of the control virus could no longer be hidden, or passed off as the ineptitude of corrupt or unsophisticated countries. We were factually and permanently bankrupt, drowned in debt after decades of destroying our productive capacity and legislating state-sponsored usury to make up the difference.

To forestall the day of reckoning we exported our financial disease to other countries, stirred up unstable regimes in the hopes that our last productive enterprise, the machinery of war, would once again distract attention from the truth of our situation. War has always been the preferred solution for bankrupt nations, simply because it is the easiest.

The institutions we relied upon to help us out of the problem were exactly the same ones that got us into it. Having rigged the economic infrastructure with financial weapons they now extorted our wages as ransom for dismantling the bombs.

This, too, was nothing new. Over the last 60 years the octopus of global financial controls that had spread its rent-seeking tentacles across the world had not only *not* prevented financial crises, it had intentionally brought them into existence. The goals of global debt organizations like the World Bank and International Monetary Fund were to foment dependency and weakness, social instability, resource terrorism and impoverishment. We experienced "more extensive and destructive crises" as Marx said, and the hard-nosed, thuggish, secretive way that our state corporatist leaders pretended to "handle" the financial terrorism was motivated, first and foremost, by a desire to "diminish the means whereby crises are prevented."

As of this writing there is still much talk in Washington about new regulations that will somehow magically prevent these crises in the future. The catch, however, is that these new regulations are being designed so that they will not, in any way, shape or form, cause even the slightest hiccup of inconvenience to those who engineered the crisis. The same politicians who are giving the economic terrorists taxpayer money, interest-free, recently defeated a tax-payer-demanded usury cap of 15% interest. (Even a politician who suggested capping interest at *30%* was also quickly silenced.)

Occasionally a sacrificial lamb was trotted out to appease the masses: a CEO was fired (with full payout, of course) or otherwise embarrassed, but the goals of both political parties and the financial terrorists were clear:

Preventing crises is never the goal of the Vyron— preventing prevention is.

The Passion of the Vyron

A few years back a Christian pornographer by the name of Mel Gibson released a movie called *The Passion of the Christ*. It was a very bad movie and would not be worth dwelling on but for the fact that it was essentially a love letter to the Vyron: two hours of nonstop simulated torture, blood, flying bits of flesh, screams, whippings and stabbings—bone-crushing sadism rendered in full Technicolor. Christians of all flavors flocked to theaters and were awed by this orgy of squirting, suppurating bodily fluids— none of which follows the scriptural descriptions of the last hours of Jesus. By comparison, *The Last Temptation of Christ*, which showed Jesus as a conflicted, flawed, and human hero, was protested

violently by millions of Christians and de-
nounced as depraved and heretical.

The success of *Passion*, especially compared
with *Temptation*, showed that for all the divisions,
sects, feuds, hair-splitting and various administra-
tive differences among the many flavors of free-
market Christianity, nothing brings competitors
together like a chance to see their prophet of
Love and Peace literally being ripped to pieces.
By looking at the success of this film, as well as
extermination fantasies like the *Left Behind* series
of books, you researchers of the future might discover that it showed a fundamental truth about
the Official Religion of America during its own
end times:

The Vyron does not love Jesus.
It loves the Crucifixion.

Few delivery systems have proven more ef-
fective over the years than the image of the Son
of God stripped, nailed and hanging bloody on a
cross. The crucifixion is Christianity's 9/11, the
Vyron's gospel of terror kept alive through endless repetition and transmission of the images of
death and suffering.

That's not to say all Christians approved of the blood-soaked fantasies of a Jew-hating alcoholic like Gibson; most Christians didn't. But the film raises a serious question: how much virus does it take to kill a person, a religion, a nation?

The Vyron has put out its call: we're in a war of civilizations, a religious war, a war to end all wars, a war for the soul of Jesus himself. We will need ever more extreme warriors if we are to defeat the darkness of non-Christianity now threatening us. And if avenging Jesus isn't strong enough motivation there is another, even better reason:

God wants us to end the world.

The fantasy of a glorious and holy global destruction is the premise of the most popular religious fantasy books in recent times, *Left Behind*. These books cast Jesus as the harbinger of mass death and destruction across the world; they advocate a message of absolute domination by and military obedience to Him.[20]

---

[20] The books, interestingly, resemble Ayn Rand's atheist fiction in certain telling ways: the heroes are rigid, self-absorbed and unempathic; they regard

To the extremists who bought these books and believe its message of mass murder via the holy and preordained Rapture, nuclear weapons are nothing more than an opportunity to bring about the Second Coming—they are, quite literally, gifts from God.

---

women as chattel; non-believers (or "non-producers" in Randian parlance) are evil scum who must be eliminated from the earth without hesitation or remorse. The books have sold an estimates 75 million copies to date.

What The Vyron Wants

> To understand this world you must know that the military establishments of the United States and the Soviet Union have united against the civilians of both countries.

> —High-level State Department official
> to John Kenneth Galbraith, 1974

You might be wondering: if the Vyron had gained so much control over our lives at the end of America, what was left for it to do? Hadn't it achieved its goals? Wasn't it happy with this victory?

The answer is no. The Vyron is never happy. The Vyron does not know what happiness is.

The Vyron has no concept of satiation or satis-
faction.

The Vyron is always
just beginning.

The small skirmishes, police actions, and
covert wars going on around the globe at any
time can never satisfy the Vyron. It demands big
results, bold actions leading to mass infection
wherever possible. It does not want the right to
commit mass murder to be the sole province of
wealthy powers, although it convinces the leaders
of those powers that that should be the case.

The Vyron knows that the ultimate delivery
device for the control virus lives beneath our soil,
hides in our mountains and oceans. The Vyron
weeps for these trapped liberators, rages at the
injustice of their captivity.

The Vyron believes that nuclear
weapons have rights too.

The Vyron killed Kennedy for refusing to
unleash these beautiful flowers of light on the
Cubans and Russians, and believes the world

would be a better place if he had. The Vyron knows that nuclear weapons are the true victims of our modern age, built and proliferated like the glorious natural phenomena they are, and that dropping them on Hiroshima and Nagasaki was the greatest event in human history as Truman said, spreading peace and stability around the globe. In order to survive in the modern age the Vyron must spread a gospel of genetic mutation, one carried not on a cross or sword but a mushroom cloud.

The Vyron is furious that we are ungrateful to our atomic savior. We have blasphemed it with talk of disarmament and non-proliferation treaties; commit a terrible injustice by depriving the world the chance to thrive under the full light of the nuclear sun. But all is not loss: more regimes are seeking these weapons and will not be held back much longer. More and more people have heard the call of the Vyron, and it is their right and their destiny to welcome it.

American politicians and their handlers are busy sharpening their pencils, performing their calculations, figuring how long it will be before they can be allowed to liberate the missiles that will save us. They know that in the last two world wars public opinion was steadfastly against both, that it took enormous effort to motivate the people to join those efforts. But oh, what successes they were! What wondrous destruction! What thrilling loss of life!

This time the shock troops of war are not yet sufficiently simplified, but they are getting that way: the Vyron has already weaponized religion to a point not seen in centuries. It already infects the minds of millions with the bloody trauma of its gospel.

The Vyron has no natural enemies; therefore it invents them.

Resisting The Vyron

Mens sana in corpore sano

Throughout history the most successful attempts to resist the control virus have come through peaceful protest. Certain brave people concluded that since the virus replicates through violence and abuse, the only way to defeat the Vyron is by civil disobedience and nonviolent demonstration. These brave souls were proven correct, but not before the Vyron had blown their heads off.

Peaceful resistance enrages the control virus, the way mass starvations, murders, firebombings, holocausts, and abused children upset the rest of us. To not allow oneself to be provoked is therefore the first step to resisting the Vyron. The provocation is usually administered by control addicts in their various disguises and can come in many forms.

How we respond to provocations from the control virus at any given time depends on many things—having a predisposition for infection, or just having a bad day are enough to allow the Vyron into our lives at least temporarily. This is because the Vyron, like any virus or other potentially deadly infection, takes root more easily in a vulnerable or comprised system. Since the Vyron looks for the path of least resistance it infects the weakest individuals first, enlisting them to spread the control virus to others.

I cannot propose a cure, but I suggest that you build resistance by examining the potential infection points in your own life and seeing if there is anything you can do to mitigate them. Remember that the Vyron operates in a very consistent, repetitive manner; once you learn to identify some of its methods you can hopefully learn to resist it.

The Vyron thrives on chaos, drama, and tragedy, and uses cover of emergency to force people into unwise or self-destructive choices.

Therefore, remaining calm in moments of crisis can buy valuable time for discerning between genuine crisis and Vyron-created chaos.

The Vyron builds a consensus of hate against others wherever possible, enlisting armies of weaker minds to infect stronger ones. In order to mask its true motives the Vyron is constantly demonizing others, waging proxy wars against the target in order to soften it for infection. This is the preferred method of the weapons marketers when creating a new war, for example, and has been used successfully for centuries.

Next, the Vyron controls the message by isolating the target from independent analysis if at all possible. Most people who engage in proxy wars against others on behalf of the Vyron are often shocked to discover—only too late—that they have been entirely misled about the nature of the enemy, usually leaving such shame and hard feelings on both sides that reconciliation is impossible.[21]

---

[21] A good example of this deception involved JFK, who campaigned on dire warnings of a "missile gap" with the USSR, only to learn once he was in office that the Soviet Union had only a tiny fraction of the potential bombs the American people had been led to believe they possessed. An outraged Kennedy then changed course on the trap set for him in the Bay of Pigs by

The Vyron always operates under one immutable law: that it is easier to destroy than to build.

Urgency, chaos, pressure, dualism, self-righteousness, victimization—the Vyron has an endless supply of tricks to enlist you into doing its bidding. Therefore wherever possible practice tolerance, cultivate complexity, employ critical thinking. Remember that although they might ask for your help, an uninfected person will never try to enlist you into fighting his or her battles; only somebody under the control of the Vyron will do that.

If you resist, calmly but firmly, the Vyron will eventually show itself by turning on you, accusing you of disloyalty, treason, betrayal, and eventually demonizing you as well. This is unfortunate but necessary; whatever pain you experience as the target of the Vyron's rage, it will enable you to get away from the virus sooner than if you stayed around. Negotiating with the Vyron invariably leads to much greater and more difficult problems later on.

Bissell and Dulles, setting off the chain of events leading to his execution two years later.

Once you know that you are in the presence of the Vyron you have no other choice but run, unless you are in a position above the Vyron and can sufficiently neutralize it—through firing, breaking up or divorce—provided you do it carefully. Remember the Vyron is a virus, and can take advantage of the smallest opening to begin the infection process all over again.

Since the Vyron lives only to replicate itself, the control addicts it uses to spread itself are likewise entirely self-absorbed, monomaniacal bullies and manipulators who expect you to focus on nothing but them, as they slowly weaken your mind and body and make you a host for the Vyron. These control addicts come in many forms and can be tremendously difficult to eradicate from one's life.

I believe that the control virus had spread so completely through society that virtually every American family now has at least one infected individual connected to it, a control addict who exercises an unhealthy and even destructive amount of control over the thoughts, behaviors, and feelings of the others. It could be one or both parents, children, siblings, grandparents, aunts or uncles. It comes in the form of abusive husbands who control their wives' every expenditure; it takes the form of the seemingly loving mothers who keep their children in constant panic with a never-ending cycle of faked illnesses; it appears in the parents who keep their children on digital leashes and militaristic regimens, controlling and monitoring their every move with such fanatical precision that childhood at the end of America was the most over-scheduled, paranoid, least free and fun it had ever been.

That brings me to my final piece of advice:

Resist Control.

Always. In all its forms.

You must learn to reject being controlled just as urgently as you must resist the urge to control others. It is an old and perennial urge, based mainly on normal fears that live deep within each of us: fear of abandonment and the need for love, primarily. It is very difficult to recognize or admit the signs of the Vyron in ourselves, although we have all been exposed and therefore still carry traces of it within us.

See if you can identify areas in your own life where the line between concern and control overlap, whether the frustrations of daily life are caused by genuine injury or simply the failure of others to conform to your own expectations. Control addicts can be masters at passive-aggression, as a way to turn the blame back onto you, so it's important to be honest and calmly distinguish the difference in your own life.

Ultimately there is no way to fully eradicate the Vyron, but with patience and practice the destructive effects can be minimized.

These steps may or may not help you to resist infection; you might find other techniques that work better for you.

Children of the future, if nothing else I can assure you that wherever you live, however far into the future and whatever your style of government, economy, religion or social mores, beware: the Vyron is still there beside you, looking over your shoulder, waiting, biding its time.

Suggested Reading

Adorno, et al. *The Authoritarian Personality.*
Brodie, Richard. *Virus Of The Mind.*
Burroughs, William S. *Naked Lunch.*
Burroughs, William S. *The Adding Machine.*
Dawkins, Richard. *The Selfish Gene.*
Hofstdater, Richard, *Anti-Intellectualism In American Life.*
Lasch, Christopher. *Culture Of Narcissism.*
Oakley, Barbara. *Evil Genes.*
Pinker, Steven. *How The Mind Works.*
Taylor, Charles. *Sources of the Self.*
Vaknin, Sam, *Malignant Self-Love: Narcissism Revisited.*

Version History

Date	Ver.	Notes
06/09	1.0	2 uncorrected proof (UP) copies (06/09)
07/09	1.1	25 first printing (fixes bugs, adds Acknowledgments and Discussion Guide, corrects cover alignment, changes back cover copy, changes to ch. 1)
07/09	1.2	1 UP, final edits for 1st printing (Lulu Rev.4)

Discussion Guide

1. The author suggests that exposure to excess trauma can lead people to either become "carriers" of the control virus (through certain personality disorders) or "shrinkers" from the control virus (soldiers with PTSD, for example). What do you think of the connection between trauma and control? Do you believe they are connected? Are there any examples in your own lives where you might have seen this connection?

2. In "Gaming The Corporative" the author argues that the corporative, or self-identifying group is far more important in our lives than we realize. What are the major corporatives you belong to in your professional and personal life? Which are most important for you personally?

3. One of the ways that groups, businesses, or even whole industries fall prey to the control virus is when they change their corporative, or business identity, without realizing it. He uses the examples of newspapers venturing into real estate and sports team speculation, and Microsoft's "embrace-extend-extinguish" strategy as two different examples of how great companies can get led astray. Can you think of other examples?

4. "A free and just society is completely incompatible with the concept of zero tolerance." (p. 63) Agree or disagree?

5. While certain religious extremism shows evidence of the control virus, the author also says that religion itself might be an early attempt to neutralize the virus, by putting ultimate control into the hands of a Higher Power. How does the presence of religious extremists alter your view or practice of religion, if at all?

About The Living Book

My goals in writing this book were twofold: first, to share these ideas with you, which I hope will help you as much as they have me; and second, to solicit your help in making my understanding of them better. That is why I call this a Living Book, to give you a chance to improve it as well as to build a memory into the book itself. I hope to update *How America Died* in future printings with new ideas, chapters, and sources, and invite you, the reader, to take part in the ongoing creation of this book. All contributors will be credited and compensated with copies of the printing in which their contributions appear. Please email timhallbooks@gmail.com for more information.